A Pup Like Fox

by Hareem Atif Khan • illustrated by Neha Rawat

Lucy Calkins and Michael Rae-Grant, Series Editors

LETTER-SOUND CORRESPONDENCES

m, t, a, n, s, p, i, d,
g, o, c, k, ck, r, u,
h, b, e, f, ff, l, ll, z,
j, w, y, x, qu, -e, -o,
-y, ch, sh, th

HIGH-FREQUENCY WORDS

is, like, see, the, has, his, too, of, says, to, for, look, you, do

A Pup Like Fox
Author: Hareem Atif Khan
Series Editors: Lucy Calkins and Michael Rae-Grant

Heinemann
145 Maplewood Avenue, Suite 300
Portsmouth, NH 03801
www.heinemann.com

Copyright © 2023 Heinemann and The Reading and Writing Project Network, LLC

All rights reserved, including but not limited to the right to reproduce this book, or portions thereof, in any form or by any means whatsoever, without written permission from the publisher. For information on permission for reproductions or subsidiary rights licensing, please contact Heinemann at permissions@heinemann.com. Heinemann's authors have devoted their entire careers to developing the unique content in their works, and their written expression is protected by copyright law. We respectfully ask that you do not adapt, reuse, or copy anything on third-party (whether for-profit or not-for-profit) lesson-sharing websites.
—Heinemann Publishers

"Dedicated to Teachers" is a trademark of Greenwood Publishing Group, LLC.

Cataloging-in-Publication data is on file with the Library of Congress.

ISBN-13: 978-0-325-13842-8

Design and Production: Dinardo Design LLC, Carole Berg, and Rebecca Anderson

Editors: Anna Cockerille and Jennifer McKenna

Illustrations: Neha Rawat

Photographs: p. 32 (top) © Ilona Tymchenko/Dreamstime; p. 32 (bottom) © Andreas Häuslbetz/Dreamstime.

Manufacturing: Gerard Clancy

Printed in the United States of America on acid-free paper
3 4 5 6 7 8 9 10 MP 28 27 26 25 24 23
January 2023 printing / PO# 4500866727

Contents

1. Fetch! 1
2. Fox Has a Bath 13
3. The Tick 23

Fetch!

"I wish I had a pup like Fox," Imran says. "Can he do tricks?"

"He can sit," Sam says.

"Can he fetch?" Imran asks.

Imran picks up a thin stick.
"Fox! Fetch!" he yells.

Fox is off in a flash!

He jumps in the pond
and swims to get the stick.

Fox runs back with the stick.

He zips past Imran and Sam.

He runs up the path to a trash can.
"Fox, no!" yells Sam.
But Fox jumps in.

Fox digs up the trash and dumps the stick in it.

"Yuck!" says Imran.

"He smells like trash."

"My mom will be so mad!" says Sam.

"It will be OK," says Imran.

"We will get him in a bath."

"Do you still wish for a pup like Fox?" Sam asks.

Fox Has a Bath

"Let's get Fox in the bath!" Sam says.

"I will fill up the tub," says Imran.

But Fox is too quick!

He runs off with a cloth.

"Get back, you mutt!" yells Sam.

Imran and Sam look for Fox.

Imran looks by the bed.

Sam looks in a bin of socks.

Imran and Sam run in and see Fox in the trash can. "Fox, no!" yells Sam.

"Ug!" says Sam.

"He smells so bad."

Imran nods and says,

"Let's get him in the bath, fast!"

Splash!

Fox is in the bath at last.

"I do wish I had a pup like Fox," says Imran.

3

The Tick

"Fox has had a bath," says Sam.
"So next, let's brush him!"

"Um...Sam?" says Imran.
"I felt a bump on his skin."

"Yuck!" says Imran. "It's a tick."

"A tick?" asks Sam.

"A tick is a bug," says Imran.

"It nips you and sucks up blood."

"Aaaa!" yells Sam. "Squish it!"

"No," says Imran.

"If we squish it, he can get sick. Let's ask Mom for help."

Pinch! Mom gets the tick off of Fox.

"Ick!" says Mom. "Let's flush it!"

Learn about...

TICKS

Warning: this is kind of gross!

Ticks are little bugs that love to suck blood. Yuck. Told you it was gross! If a tick wants a snack, it will go questing. When a tick goes *questing,* it climbs up a plant, sticks out its front legs, and waits. Then, when an animal passes by, the tick grabs on.

Next, the tick bites through the animal's skin and sucks its blood. The tick's body fills up big and puffy, like a balloon. When it's all full, the tick drops off, *plop!*

It doesn't hurt when a tick bites. The animal can't even feel it. But some ticks carry *diseases,* or germs, that make animals sick. Ticks can make people sick too, so if you go walking in a forest where ticks live, cover up and check your skin for ticks afterward.

Talk about...

Ask your reader some questions like...

- What happened in this book?
- Is Fox a well-behaved puppy? Why or why not?
- Taking care of a puppy is a *lot* of work. What are some ways that Imran and Sam took care of Fox in this book?
- Would *you* want a pup like Fox?